GET YOUR L.I.F.E. TOGETHER

The Ultimate Guide To Building Generational Wealth With Life Insurance.

COURTNEY BECKLES

Get Your L.I.F.E Together

Copyright © 2023 by Courtney Beckles

ISBN: 9798397059039

All rights reserved. No portion of this book may be used or reproduced by any means, graphic, electronic, or mechanical, including photocopying, recording, taping, or by any information storage retrieval system, without the written permission of the publisher except in the case of brief quotations embodied in critical articles and reviews.

Foreword

Welcome to an extraordinary journey that will illuminate the path to financial security and generational wealth. In this book, author Courtney Beckles unravel the mysteries surrounding life insurance and unveil its remarkable potential as a tool for building a long-lasting legacy.

Life insurance is often seen as a safety net for our loved ones, but it holds so much more. Through clear explanations and practical strategies, Mr. Beckles will guide you on a simplified journey of understanding. You will discover how life insurance can be a powerful instrument in creating generational wealth, securing your family's future, and leaving a lasting impact.

From protecting assets and ensuring financial stability to maximizing tax advantages and funding dreams, the possibilities are within your reach. Mr. Beckles will share real-life examples of individuals who have harnessed the power of life insurance to build a strong financial foundation for their families.

It is an honor to write the foreword for "Get Your L.I.F.E. Together" by my good friend, Courtney Beckles. His exceptional knowledge, compassion, and dedication to helping others make him a true authority in the field of life insurance. I am confident that readers will find his insights invaluable and transformative, and I eagerly recommend this book to anyone who is committed to building a legacy, and creating a fulfilled, prosperous life for themselves, and their family. Prepare to be inspired, enlightened, and empowered as you embark on this life-changing journey with Mr. Beckles as your guide. Take charge of your life by reading this book. The time to prepare yourself for a shift of your mindset and wealth is now! Join Mr. Beckles as he unlocks the secrets and empower you to make informed decisions. With this book as your companion, you will gain the knowledge and confidence to navigate the realm of life insurance and embark on a path toward generational wealth. Let us begin this transformative journey together!

Michael Johnson, Mayor of Haledon, New Jersey

Contents

FOREWORD III

PART 1 LIFE INSURANCE BASICS ....

    CHAPTER 1 – WHAT IS LIFE INSURANCE 1
    CHAPTER 2 – TYPES OF LIFE INSURNACE 9
        Term Life Insurance 9
        Permanent Life Insurance 11
        Whole Life Insurance 14
        Universal Life Insurance 16
    CHAPTER 3 – HOW TO QUALIFY FOR LIFE INSURNACE 21
    CHAPTER 4 – HOW TO CALCULATE THE AMOUNT OF LIFE INSURANCE YOU NEED 27
    CHAPTER 5 – DEFINITIONS & KEY CONCEPTS 31
    CHAPTER 6 – POLICY PROVISIONS, RIDERS, OPTIONS, AND EXCLUSIONS 37
        Riders 39
        Options 41
        Exclusions 44

PART 2 ADVANCE STRATEGIES ....

    CHAPTER 7 – POLICY OWNERS RIGHTS 47
    CHAPTER 8 – CASH VALUE & POLICY LOANS 53
    CHAPTER 9 – TAX ADVANTAGES OF LIFE INSURANCE 61
    CHAPTER 10 – THE INFINITE BANKING CONCEPT 67
    CHAPTER 11 – USING LIFE INSURANCE FOR RETIREMENT INCOME 79
    CHAPTER 12 – USING LIFE INSURANCE FOR WEALTH TRANSFER 91

ABOUT THE AUTHOR 97

PART 1
LIFE INSURANCE BASICS

Chapter 1

What is Life Insurance

Life insurance is a contract between an insurance company and a policyholder, in which the insurance company guarantees payment of a death benefit to a named beneficiary or beneficiaries upon the death of the insured. The policyholder will pay a premium in a monthly, quarterly, semi-annually, or annual basis; in exchange for this guaranteed death benefit. Life insurance can also be described as any immediate estate. In other words, the death benefit is paid out, tax free to the named beneficiary or beneficiaries, without passing through probate court. The death benefit can be paid out in one large lump sum, or in installments. The policyholder gets to choose the way in which the death benefit is paid out. If no choice was made, then the beneficiary can decide.

There are five parties to a life insurance contract. The insurer, the insured, the policy owner, the payor, and the beneficiary.

1. The **insurer** is the life insurance company who takes on the risk of insuring an individual's life.

2. The **Insured** is the person's life for whom the life insurance is being bought on, and must prove insurability; meaning they must be healthy enough for the insurance company to take them on as a risk.

3. The **policy owner** is the person or entity that has policy owners' rights such as choosing the beneficiary or beneficiaries, borrowing from or against the policy, choosing settlement options, having non-forfeiture options, and so forth and so on. The policy owner's rights will be discussed in detail in a later chapter.

4. The **payor** is the person or entity that will be responsible for paying the policy premiums.

5. The **beneficiary** or beneficiaries are the person(s) or entity that will receive the death benefit.

In most cases, the insured, the policy owner, and the payor are the same person. However, this is not necessarily always the case. The policy owner and the insured could be different, and in this case, it is called a third-party ownership. For example, a man may put life insurance on his wife as the insured while he is the policy owner, and he would have the policy owner's rights. As mentioned earlier, the insured must prove evidence of insurability at the time of the application. In other words, he or she must prove that they are an acceptable risk to the insurance company in terms of health and lifestyle. The applicant must prove the ability to pay the policy that is being applied for. The insured's health and lifestyle are assessed and underwritten by the insurance company to protect them against adverse selections or adverse risks. The financial information of the applicant is assessed and underwritten by the insurance company to protect the applicant from the likeliness of not being able to afford the policy being applied for.

In the insurance business, fair discrimination is a necessary component for insurance companies to remain profitable. For a life insurance contract to be valid, it must have four components. These are an offer and acceptance, consideration, legal purpose, and competent parties.

1. An **offer** is when an insured or an applicant applies for the policy with the first premium payment. The information given on an application, along with the first premium payment is considered an offer. Acceptance is when the insurance company decides to accept the policy and issue it. Should the insurance company accept an offer, they will issue the policy on a take it or leave it basis. The applicant plays no part in constructing the contract.

2. **Consideration** on the applicant's part is the information given in the application, along with the premium payment in exchange for consideration on the insurance company's part for the promise to pay the death benefit.

3. **Legal purpose** means the contract must be constructed for a legal purpose or reason. If it is put together for an illegal reason or illegal actions were taken, then the contract is invalid.

4. **Competent parties** mean that all parties must be of legal age and show that they are fully capable of doing everything that needs to be done. For example, if it was found that the applicant was under the influence of drugs or alcohol while filling out the application, then the contract would be invalid.

Now that we have a basic understanding of life insurance let us now discuss why it is such a very important financial vehicle to have.

I believe life insurance is the most underutilized financial vehicle in our society today. Even though it has so many great financial benefits for families and provides a lot of protection, many people still do not get it. Unlike auto insurance, homeowners' insurance, and liability insurance, which are usually made mandatory by the government, life insurance is not. And, unfortunately, human being tends not to act, unless they are forced to do so. According to bankrate.com, in 2022, 106 million Americans were either without life insurance or underinsured. The main reasons why people do not get life insurance are:

- they think it costs too much,

- they are misinformed about life insurance,

- they do not have a good understanding of it,

- or they are just procrastinating.

Let us look at each of those reasons.

1. Price is one of the biggest reasons why people stay away from life insurance. Based on their experiences, or things they have heard, they may think it is very expensive, but they do not understand that there is an option for every income level. The key is to figure out what you can reasonably afford without affecting your daily lifestyle, and have that figure when you speak with an agent or broker, and make sure they design a policy that you can work with. It is important to start from where you are at financially, and you can always add more later. Also, whenever you wait around, it gets more expensive as you grow older, so you get the least expensive price when you are younger. Due to this "war" in the financial services industry, many times people who sell other products or are advocates of other products speak negatively about life insurance because they believe in other financial vehicles. I think that is the wrong approach to have because the fact is, there is a space for each financial product when someone is constructing their "financial house." It does not have to be one or the other. It can be both or all. And unfortunately, many people are easily influenced. Instead of doing their own research, they go by what someone else tells them.

2. In today's world, with the internet and social media, there are so many different influencers that are speaking on life insurance, and sometimes it confuses people because there is so much information out there. How does an uninformed individual know who to listen to? Unfortunately, when people are confused, instead of inquiring more, and taking a deeper

dive in and asking more questions, they tend to move away from it.

3. Procrastination is also a major cause for the lack of life insurance. As I mentioned before, because life insurance is not mandatory, people tend not to give it the priority it deserves. They do not see it as a priority or something that they do need right away. And because of that, it ends up getting pushed to the wayside. What usually happens is when they do have a need for it, it is very late and they cannot qualify or it may become a lot more expensive than if they had done it earlier. Do not procrastinate. Make it a point to get life insurance as early as possible.

Now, what about the people who are strong believers in life insurance and make sure they are protected? What is it that they know that others do not? People who get life insurance usually get it for one of the following reasons; income protection, mortgage protection, to take care of their funeral expenses, debt protection to satisfy their debts when they die, for their children's education, for estate planning, and wealth transfer. I will take a deeper dive into these reasons when I discussed the types of insurance in the following chapter. Before I take a deep dive into the different types of life insurance, it is important that I explain to you why I personally think life insurance is very beneficial.

First, it is not an equal exchange of value. For more permanent solutions, if you pay your premiums, life insurance will always pay you back a lot more than you put in. And for more temporary solutions this is possible as well, even though it is not guaranteed. However, you do have the peace of mind knowing that God forbid something did happen to you, your family will be protected and that money will go to whoever you want it to go to and do whatever you want to do with it. I have created a document that covers the 7 biggest misconceptions about life insurance and what the truths really are.

Scan the QR Code OR go to the link below to get this free document.

https://docs.google.com/document/d/1b66LhM7tdwXKhxXFANGt Iqrx57ZctkLkJ5KnsxefnWA/edit?usp=sharing

Let us take for example, a thirty-year-old male, the policy premium is $30 per month; and he has a policy with a death benefit of $300,000. If he only paid into that policy for three years, that will be a total payment of $1,080. he died after three years, his beneficiary would get $300,000, even though he only funded the policy with $1,080. I do not know any other financial vehicle that does anything like this. That money will go to his named beneficiary to use however it's intended to be used, without going through probate court; and it is 100% tax free!

In most states, the death benefit is also protected against creditors. Therefore, they would not be able to access nor sue the beneficiary for any of that money. Even if the debt is legitimately owed. The death benefit can be paid out in one lump sum, or it could be paid out in installments. The policy owner would have the option to choose that during the time of owning the policy, however, if the option was not selected, then the beneficiary or beneficiaries have the option to choose however they want the cash to be dispersed.

Let us now look at the different types of life insurance; illustrate the pros and cons of each; discuss the features and benefits; and cover the different purposes of each type.

Chapter 2

Types of Life Insurance

There are two main types of life insurance. There is term life insurance and permanent life insurance. Term Life insurance is a temporary solution for temporary needs, and permanent life insurance is a solution for long term needs and concerns.

Term Life Insurance

Term Life insurance is the purest form of life insurance, because you get the maximum amount of death benefit for the least amount of premiums paid. The purpose of Term Life insurance is to give you maximum protection in your earlier years; prior to you earning enough cash, or have enough assets to protect you and your family in the event of your untimely death. As time passes and your income grows, your children grow up, and there is no longer a need for you to take care of them; the need for term life insurance goes away. As you can see, these are temporary needs and concerns.

I have seen many people describe term life insurance as being like paying rent. However, I disagree with that analogy because this product is far more superior, and way more significant of a product than paying rent. It is not comparable. At no point during the time a person rents an apartment or a house or whatever dwelling they live in, does their family get a lump sum or an immediate estate if they die during the time they are living there.

For example, if you are a 25-year-old male, and you need half a million dollars worth of life insurance, and let us say your premium payment is $30 per month and you only made those payments for two years. And God forbid you died in two years. Your beneficiary will be paid out half a million dollars. That is $500,000 and you only paid premium of two years which in total is only $720. So, you paid $720 Within two years and your family receives $500,000. I cannot think of another financial vehicle you can put money in that can give you that kind of immediate return.

Obviously, there is nothing in renting that compares to anything like term life insurance. Therefore, I think they should not be compared. Instead, I call Term Life Insurance the "what if I die" type of life insurance. In other words, what if I die before my children grow up? I want to make sure that there is enough money to take care of them and my spouse. I want to make sure that there is enough money to replace my income for three years, five years, or ten years, or the most my budget can afford to pay for. This will enable them to continue living without financial stress until they have adjusted to living without my income. What if I die before my mortgage is paid off? I want to make sure that my family does not have the hassle or stress of paying for the mortgage, having to move, or being forced to sell the house. Even though my income would no longer be available, my life insurance would pay off the house so my family do not have to worry about it. What if I die before my children go to college? My income would not be there to help so I want to make sure that I have money to support or help them with their college education.

As you can see these are all temporary needs, during a certain period. That is why term life insurance is the perfect solution for taking care of these concerns. Term life insurance is usually sold in periods of 10, 20, or 30 years. However, some companies offer unusual options such as 5, 15, or 25 years' term policies.

It is important to note that in most cases, if the insured does not die within the specified term, the policy ends without any return of premiums paid. Permanent life insurance is there to take care of your long-term goals and your long-term needs. Similarly, to how term insurance is compared to renting. I have also seen many individuals referring to permanent life insurance as like owning a house. Again, this is misstating the power of a permanent life insurance policy.

Permanent Life Insurance

A permanent life insurance policy is way more superior and is a more valuable asset than owning a house. Let me explain.

There are two reasons why I believe a permanent life insurance policy should not be compared to owning a home. Firstly, a house is valued at what the market dictates. In other words, houses are valued based on how much people are willing to pay for that house in the current market regardless of how much you paid for it. For example, you could have paid $600,000 for a home in March 2021. However, two years later, in March 2023, that same exact house could be valued at $400,000. By no fault of your own, nor any damage you did to devalue the house. The only thing that is different is just that the market is not willing to pay more than $400,000 in March of 2023. The price of that house is not determined by how much work you put into it, how much the material you use costs, and the sweat equity you put into it. If buyers are not willing to pay what you are asking, then the house is not valued at a penny more than what a buyer is willing to pay in the current market.

This is not the case with a permanent life insurance policy. If you pay your premium, the value of your policy will only go up, and it will continue to go up. It will not go down at all. The only exception will be if you are invested in a variable product, which I will explain further later in the chapter.

The other major factor is you do not truly own the house until you are completely paid off on it. For example, if you have a 30-year mortgage and you have made 15 years of payment on that mortgage, if things got bad and you are no longer able to afford to make the mortgage payment, the only good solution for you would be to sell the house for more than what you owe on it; which at that point you should have some equity in the house. But again, it would have to be for more than what you owe in order to benefit from it. Otherwise, that 15 years of payment that you have invested in that house could go for nothing. That house could be foreclosed on, and the bank could take the house away from you even though you have paid 15 years into that 30-year mortgage.

Unfortunately, many people faced a similar situation like this and ended up walking away with nothing because they were not able to sell the house, did not want to sell the house, or were not able to sell that house for more than they owe on the house; even though they had made 15 years of payment. This is not the case with a permanent life insurance policy. If you paid 15 years into a permanent life insurance policy, you have built up enough cash value in that policy whereas if you wanted to discontinue that policy, you would be paid out the cash value minus any taxes or any penalties for early surrender. However, you would not walk away with nothing; you would walk away with the value of the policy, minus any penalties and taxes that you must pay. This is a totally different from a scenario with your house. Instead, I call permanent life insurance the "when I die" type of life insurance. In other words, when I die, I want to make sure that my outstanding debts are taken care of with my policy. This avoids my family the burden of being responsible for my debts. When I die, I want to make sure that my estate is properly managed. Therefore, I would leave directions to use funds from my life insurance policy to properly manage my estate. When I die, I want to make sure that my funeral costs are all taken care of. This saves my family the embarrassment of doing Go Fund Me and being burdened with taking care of the costs of my funeral. When I die this is how I want my wealth to be distributed amongst my heirs. As you can see, these are all long term or permanent solutions. Therefore, this is what you would set up a permanent life insurance policy for; to take care of these long-term concerns and needs.

There are two types of permanent life insurance. They are whole life and universal life. And within each type, there are two forms available to you which are index and variable. Let us break down each type of permanent life insurance, as well as the different forms that they are available in.

Whole Life Insurance

Whole Life insurance is the first type of permanent life insurance and it is the most straightforward and most simple form of permanent life insurance. It offers a guaranteed death benefit for your entire life and usually has a level premium payment over a limited period, or you can pay for your entire life. The death benefit, however, protects you for your entire life. Like all permanent life insurance policies, whole life insurance has two premium payment components. I call them premium buckets. In other words, when you pay your premium, some money goes into the bucket for the cost of insurance and the rest of the money goes into the bucket for what is called the Cash Value.

I compare whole life insurance and all permanent life insurance to a bank account. A checking account and a savings account are the most popular and commonly used accounts in a bank. The checking account is where you usually pay your bills and all your expenses. In a whole life policy, this is equivalent to the cost of the insurance bucket. When you pay your premium, the part of your premium that goes into the cost of the insurance bucket, which takes care of the cost of the death benefit, and all fees associated with the policy. The remaining premium goes into the cash value bucket like a savings account in a bank, it will grow and earn interest. These components make whole life insurance a very attractive vehicle for someone that wants a guaranteed death benefit for the rest of their life while paying a level premium that does not increase and safely earning a much better return than what you can get in the bank. Two other major advantages are liquidity and tax advantages. You can access the cash value in your policy at any time, tax free without any penalties. You can also earn interest in your cash value bucket tax free and your death benefit will be passed on to your named beneficiary tax free.

The two main disadvantages of a whole life policy are it is more expensive than term insurance and it has a lot less flexibility than other permanent life insurance policies. Since the policy is there to protect you for your entire life and it also builds cash value, it is expected that it would be a lot more expensive than a term policy which is just pure death benefit and coverage ends at the end of the term. As also mentioned earlier, it is more straightforward and provides very little flexibility in terms of the premium payment and the death benefit.

An index whole life is not a very popular product; however, it does exist. I have only seen this product with mutual companies, which are insurance companies that are owned by the policy owners. In this policy, you still get to your guaranteed rate credited to you. A portion or all the remaining non-guaranteed dividend can then be tied to an index, such as the S&P 500, for the potential of higher gains. For example, one of the companies I used has a total rate of 5.75%. 3% is guaranteed, then the policy owner has the option to tie all or a portion of the remainder 2.75% non-guaranteed rate to the index. I will cover more in detail how indexing works when I explain Index Universal Life. As mentioned earlier, whole life products also offer a limited pay option while covering you for your entire life. The most common options are 10 pay, 20 pay, and pay to 65. This means premium payment is due for 10 years, 20 years, or until the insured turns age 65. Once the payment period is over, no additional payments can be made. The policy owner cannot decide to continue making payments. The premium payment must follow the limited pay policy structure as originally designed.

Universal Life Insurance

Unlike whole life insurance, a universal life insurance policy provides flexibility in premiums and death benefits. The policy owner can choose the amount and frequency of premiums as well as adjust the death benefit up and down. As changes and circumstances in their lives occurs. It provides great flexibility and will remain in force for the insured's entire life if policy premium minimums are paid timely. Universal Life is also available in two forms, which are indexed universal life and variable universal life. An indexed universal life policy, also known as an IUL gives you the flexibility of a regular universal life policy with the added benefit of having your cash value tied to an index in the market. This type of strategy gives the policy owner the potential of earning a lot more in interest meanwhile protecting them against the downside of the market. This is done by having a ceiling and a floor. The ceiling caps the interest that the policy owner can earn based on the gain of the index that they are tied to, such as the S&P 500 or Bloomberg index. For example, if the index that you selected went up 20% but the cap is 12% you would earn 12% on your cash value. If the index went up 8% you would earn 8%. So, it gives you up to the maximum of the cap and if it is if the interest earned is within that cap, you would earn that interest but if it is over the cap, then the cap is what you earn. The floor is usually 0% interest. If the market went down, your loss will be nothing. You would just not gain anything unlike a variable product where you are invested in the market.

In an IUL, you are tied to the index of your choosing, but you are not invested in the market. Therefore, you do not lose any of your cash value when the market goes. You just lose the ability to gain any interest. If you had a great gain one year, let us say you had $100,000 in cash value and you gain 10%, your new principal will be $110,000, and in the next year, let us say the market went down. You will be locked in at $110,000. You would not lose anything from the $110,000 that you already have. Some life insurance companies offer an uncapped index, which means that if the index goes up 30% or 40%, you would be able to get all those gains. However, the drawback to that is it requires a certain percentage of your account value to be paid to the life insurance company. Unlike whole life, index universal life policies do not offer a guarantee. The interest you are credited is based on the performance of the indexes that you are tied to, and since no one can predict the market, there is no guaranteed rate. However, here are three ways you can guarantee that you never get zero interest credited in your IUL policy.

First, you can decide not to be tied to an index. Since you can make your interest crediting options year to year, which is called one-year point to point selection. For example, if the policy starts on February 1, you are locked into your selections until January 31st of the following year. Your new selections would start on February 1st of the following year. You can choose to not be tied to any index and ask the company to give you your guaranteed credit from the fixed account like you do in the whole life insurance.

Secondly, you can diversify your options meaning you can opt to be tied to multiple indexes by splitting up your percentages like 20% in each index. It is recommended that you also include the fixed account in your percentage breakdown.

Thirdly, you can choose what is called the rate lock option. Again, since it is one-year point to point selection from the beginning of the year to the end of the policy year, you can select a rate you like anytime within the year and lock in that rate.

Let us say your policy began and February 1 of 2023, and in July 2023 the index was at 10%, and you locked in at 10%. On January 31st of 2024, if the rate is lower than 10%, you would have gotten the 10% that you locked in July. However, if the rate finished higher than 10%, you lost the potential of gaining more interest. Bottom line, along with the flexibility of premium payments and death benefit, an IUL gives you the potential to gain a lot more in interest while protecting you from losing any of your principal.

A variable universal life policy, otherwise known as VUL, is a universal life policy where the cash value is invested in the stock market. The advantages are that it provides you with the flexibility, as all universal life policy does for the premium payment as well as the death benefit, and you are able to earn a lot more in interest due to the cash value being invested in the stock market. The policy owner can choose where they want the money to go. So, that gives them some control in determining how their policy grows. The disadvantage obviously is the risk that is associated with it being that it is invested in the stock market, it can also lose value. And as a result of the policy losing value, the death benefit could also be reduced.

It is important to note that variable products are also regulated by the SEC, which is the Securities and Exchange Commission. Because they are securities, a life insurance producer will also need securities license in order to sell any variable life insurance product. I am not a big fan of variable life insurance products because I think it takes away from the core value of life insurance, which is to provide a guaranteed death benefit and grow your money safely and uninterruptedly. In any case, if a variable life insurance product is attractive to you, make sure that you speak with an insurance professional that is very experienced in selling variable products. Make sure you understand all the risks and make sure that you are knowledgeable enough to make educated decisions when deciding where your money goes in this cash value bucket.

Now that we understand the benefits of life insurance and we understand the different types of life insurance, let us look at how you go about qualifying to get a life insurance policy.

Follow the link or scan QR Code below for a YouTube video explaining the difference between term life insurance and permanent life insurance.

https://youtu.be/nuNqi12ksGM

Chapter 3

How to Qualify for Life Insurance

In order to qualify for life insurance, you must pass medical underwriting, lifestyle underwriting, and financial underwriting. Life Insurance companies must do their due diligence to make sure that the persons being insured are acceptable risks before taking them on as insureds. Fair discrimination is a necessary part of the life insurance business. Life insurance companies must exercise fair discrimination in order to stay profitable and to stay in business. Fair discrimination is exercised by insurance companies in order to protect themselves from adverse risks. Therefore, applicants can be denied based on their poor health condition, their reckless lifestyle, or if they are not financially competent to handle the policy they are applying for.

Adverse risks are risks that will likely result in a loss or have a very, very high chance of resulting in a loss. You can imagine an insurance company would not be in business for long if they take on too many of these risks. Now that we understand this fact, let us examine the process of applying for life insurance. When an applicant applies for life insurance, the information given on the application is what is called field underwriting. This is the first level of underwriting. The insurance company takes the information given by the applicant to an agent or a broker and uses it to help underwrite the applicant. During the application intake process, questions are asked about the insured medical history, about their lifestyle, and about their financial situation. In most cases, a physical exam or a medical exam is also performed by the insurance company. In this exam, the insured will have to do a blood and urine sample, take their blood pressure, as well as measure their height and weight. Some insurance companies will allow you to get a policy without doing a medical exam up to a certain dollar amount. In these policies, the rates are usually a little higher than if you had done a full medical. Some major medical concerns are preexisting conditions such as cancer, heart disease, stroke, diabetes, high blood pressure, HIV or AIDS, mental health conditions such as depression or bipolar disorder, high cholesterol, obesity, any type of genetic disorder, or family-related health history. Disorders with a major organ such as the bladder, intestines, kidney, spleen, stomach, lungs, or liver usually are a cause for concern as well. Any preexisting conditions usually lead to further questioning to get full details. After careful consideration, the insurance company usually comes back with an acceptance at a higher premium rate or a denial. It is important to be very honest and truthful about your medical history or conditions if you lie the insurance company will find out.

The life insurance companies use an organization called the Medical Information Bureau or MIB. This is an organization that is owned by life insurance companies in which they share medical and consumer information. If you were denied for life insurance in the past because of medical reasons, the MIB would be informed. When applying for life insurance, you must agree to have your consumer report checked. If you decline to have your consumer report checked, then your application will be denied. Your lifestyle is also a big factor in determining your qualification for life insurance. At the top of the list are tobacco use, alcohol or drug use, and risky occupations or hobbies. Tobacco use is a major factor in determining your life insurance rate. As a matter of fact, rating classes start at whether you are a tobacco user or not. However, it is not a reason to be denied, you would just have to pay more if you regularly use tobacco in any form. If you are just a tobacco user without any other condition, then you can just expect to pay more than a non-tobacco user. Drug and alcohol use or abuse is another concern of a life insurance company. Obviously, if a person is a drug or an alcohol abuser, it is more likely that that person can do something that is dangerous that could cause them to die. Insurance companies carefully examine your use of drugs and alcohol to determine if it is acceptable based on the frequency that you drink or use drugs.

It is important to note that even though an AA program is there to help people with drug or alcohol abuse, it does not help you when applying for life insurance. It is looked at in a negative way. I compare this to a debt relief company in the credit industry. If you work with a debt relief company that helps you reduce your debt for a fraction of what you owe, future creditors will consider this a weakness or strike against you. They would look at it as you're not being responsible enough to take care of your own debt. You are working with a debt relief company to help you reduce and eliminate some of your debts is seen as a red flag to them; and they would not want to lend you any money going forward. In life insurance, the AA program for alcoholics is looked at in the same manner. In other words, you were not responsible enough to manage your own habits therefore, you needed help to do that so they look at that as a red flag. And as a result, that may cause you to be denied. Your driving record is another thing that is looked at. They look at the points that you have on your driver's license abstract, especially for moving violations. They look at if you had any DUI, or anything of that nature. In other words, drivers that have a lot of moving violations or records of driving dangerously are more likely to do something that can cause them to die while driving.

Risky jobs such as pilots, active military workers, oil workers, first responders, construction workers, workers that work in a war zone or work in a country that is most likely to be in war are all considered high risks. These types of jobs are looked at very carefully when being underwritten and underwriters are likely to ask a lot of questions to get a full detail of what the job entails and what is the day-to-day operation of the insured to determine if this is a risk worth taking or not.

Risky hobbies include hobbies such as skydiving, bungee jumping, racecar driving, scuba diving, hang gliding, rock climbing, hiking, and private piloting. Like risky jobs, underwriters will ask follow-up questions to find out how often these activities are being practiced, how recently they have been practiced, and what are the plans to participate in the activities soon; to determine if this is a risk worth taking or not. Each life insurance company has its own risk tolerance. Therefore, you should not automatically assume anything before getting the information. However, it is important to have a general idea of what life insurance companies are looking at so you know what to expect.

In doing financial underwriting, the life insurance company looks at the answers given to the financial questions asked on the application. Some important numbers that they look at are the applicant's salary, their net worth, their assets, and their available liquid cash on hand. The company reviews these numbers to protect themselves and to protect the applicant from getting a policy they cannot afford. They want to make sure that the coverage applied for is suitable for the applicant and it makes sense with their financial needs. Typically, an insurance company will allow you to get 10, 15, 20, 25, or 30 times your yearly salary in coverage, depending on your age. If you are older, then it is a smaller number of years available. If you are under 35 years old, then you are more likely to be able to buy 30 times your yearly salary. As mentioned earlier, affordability is also a concern. For example, if you have a net worth of $15,000, liquid cash on hand of $10,000, yearly salary of less than $100,000, with a policy premium payment of $25,000 per year for ten years, you can expect to be questioned. The insurance company would probably come back and say it does not fit their suitability guidelines. If you adjust the numbers, then most likely documentation would be requested to support your claim. Remember, it is important to be honest and accurate with your statements to the best of your knowledge.

In saying all this, I would like to close out this chapter with a final thought. Nothing happens until you get moving. Do not automatically assume that you do not qualify for life insurance because you have a previously pre-existing medical condition or some type of medical disorder. Get out there and find the companies that will still insure you with your conditions. There are agents and brokers that specialize in these types of policies for people with preexisting conditions. Sometimes these policies are automatically same day approval up to a certain amount of death benefit.

So do not be lazy. Gather all the information and do your research. Find out what you qualify for and find out what you can afford. Then determine how you can move forward. Always remember it is better to have some life insurance rather than having no life insurance at all.

For more information, go to the YouTube link or scan QR code below for a short video on this topic.

https://youtu.be/ByawtRnk44g

Chapter 4

How to Calculate the Amount of Life Insurance You Need

There are many ways to determine how much life insurance you need to protect your family. However, we will focus on the two most used methods of figuring out this number. The human life value and the L.I.F.E. method are the two main ways to calculate how much life insurance an individual need.

Human life value method is based around the breadwinner's income. It considers the remaining working years of the breadwinner and multiplies those years by their yearly salary. For example, if the breadwinner is 35 years old, and they are expected to work until they are 65 years old and retire at that age, then they would receive 30 years of protection. Therefore, they will multiply their yearly salary by 30 years. If they were 45 years old and expected to retire at 65, then they will multiply their yearly salary by 20 years. Some advisors will help you determine your need for protection based on this simple calculation, while others will take other factors into consideration to get a more accurate number. Other factors include the after-tax dollars, meaning the net dollars received as income, not the gross payroll dollars, self-maintenance dollars, anticipated salary increases, and also inflation. Let us look at each of these factors. To get a more accurate dollar amount for needs or protection you can figure out your gross income minus the taxes that you would pay.

For example, if you made $70,000 per year and your taxes are at 30%, then your yearly net income would be $49,000. Therefore, your starting point would be $49,000 per year, not $70,000 per year. You can then determine how much of that $49,000 would be used for self-maintenance or self-care for the breadwinner. Since the breadwinner would not be alive anymore, there wouldn't be a need to spend any money on him or her. Therefore, that would be subtracted from that $49,000. Let's say the breadwinner normally would use 20% of their net income for self-care and self-maintenance. That $49,000 will now be down to $39,200. I am not very familiar with the salary increases or wage increases are these days. However, let us say for argument's sake, that the salary increase is at 2% salary per year. The first year's increase at 2% will be $39,984, your new net salary will be $39,984 in the first year, then you would add 2% onto that new total for each year and increase the net salary each year by keep adding 2% to the new total. You would then take inflation into consideration and add the inflation amount. Let's say you want to use an average of 3% for inflation, you would find out 3% of the $39,984 and add that 3%. Then you would do that each year to get to your final number. That final number would be a more accurate representation of the family's needs without you. Sometimes individuals find that final number to be a very large amount of insurance and they find it unaffordable based on their current financial situation. In this case, they would make an adjustment and instead of doing your entire life value, they would reduce it to a certain number of years to give the family enough time to adjust to living without your income. This may be three years, five years, or ten years, or whatever is most affordable. However, the starting point will be going for the maximum amount, then you can work your way back if it ends up being unaffordable.

The next method to determine how much life insurance you need is the L.I.F.E. method. L.I.F.E. is an acronym for loans, income, final expense, and education.

- **L**oans, which represent any debt you owe such as mortgage, auto loans, student loans, credit card debt, etc.

- **I**ncome takes into consideration the number of years the insured would want his or her income to be available during the adjustment period, whether that may be three, five or ten years. The income may be calculated as gross income or net income for a more accurate number.

- **F**inal expenses. All costs associated with your funeral arrangements should be added up here.

- **E**ducation, which is your children's education. You want to account for $100,000 per child in this area for a four-year college.

After adding up all these totals, you would then subtract the value of all liquid assets, which may include cash, stocks, bonds, mutual funds, retirement savings, etc. The difference between the two totals would be the total need for life insurance. The L.I.F.E. may also be explained in the form of the D.I.M.E. acronym. **D** represents all your debts and final expenses. **I** is for income, **M** is for mortgage, and **E** is for education.

Regardless of which method you use. The key thing to understand is that it is your number. These methods are guidelines that give you a frame in which to work within. As long as you can reasonably show the need for the amount of coverage, and you qualify medically and financially, an insurance company would usually approve you for the coverage applied for. When working with an agent or broker, be sure to clearly communicate your needs and goals so they can tailor your policy specifically for you.

Go to the link or scan QR code below for a visual explaining this topic.

https://youtu.be/m-RLI6IVzgk

Chapter 5

Definitions & Key Concepts

In this chapter, I will discuss definitions and key concepts that I think you need to understand about life insurance. These definitions and concepts will enable you to have a conversation with an agent or broker at a higher level. Understanding them would enable you to make the agent or brokers job easier as well as make the process smoother for you as an educated consumer. The first thing I will cover is the five parts of a life insurance contract. These are the insurer, the insured, the policy owner, the payor, and the beneficiary.

- The **insurer** is the life insurance company that is taking on the risk of paying the death benefit when the insured dies.

- The **insured** is the person's life that the insurance policy is on. They would have to prove Evidence of Insurability before the policy is issued.

- The **policy owner** is the person that has policy owners' rights on the policy and can make decisions on the policy. Sometimes this is the insured and in other cases, it is a third-party owner. I will cover policy owners' rights in detail in a later chapter.

- The **payor** of the policy is the person that will pay the premium for the policy. This could be the insured, or it could be another person or entity.

- The **beneficiary** is the person or entity that will receive the death benefit when the insured dies. It is important to note that only the insured must be a real person. The beneficiary, payor, and policy owner could be a person or an entity.

Now that we have covered the five main parts of a life insurance contract, let us look at some other key definitions that you should know if you want to be miles ahead of the average person buying life insurance.

Premium - Premium is the amount of money you pay to keep the policy in force. It can be paid on an annual, semiannual, quarterly, or monthly basis.

Insurability - Insurability is what the insured must prove prior to the policy being issued in order to be considered as an acceptable risk by the insurance company. This includes health and lifestyle assessment.

Insurable Interest – Insurable interest must be proven during the application process. The policy owner or applicant must prove that there will be a financial loss to the beneficiary if the insured dies.

Producer - A life insurance producer is a person who solicits and negotiates life insurance products. A producer can be an agent, broker, or consultant. An agent is a producer that represents a life insurance company he or she is contracted with. Usually, an agent is only allowed to write policies for the company they represent. A broker does not represent a particular life insurance company. The broker has access to many different life insurance carriers, and they represent the client or prospect. A consultant represents either a life insurance company, an individual or company.

Face Amount – The face amount is the total amount of death benefit that the beneficiary will receive when the insured dies.

Underwriting - Underwriting is the insurance company's process of assessing risks after they receive an application. Typically, the insurance company will do medical underwriting, lifestyle underwriting, and financial underwriting. This process helps the life insurance company from taking on adverse risks.

Representation - Representations are statements an applicant made in a life insurance application that at the time, are correct, to the best of their knowledge.

Warranties - Warranties are factual statements given by an insured or an applicant during the application process. If these statements are found to be untrue, this could void the insurance policy.

Replacement - Replacement in life insurance is when a policy owner surrender or lapse a current policy and replace it with a new life insurance policy.

Stock Insurer – a stock insurer is an insurance company that is owned by shareholders or stockholders and is traded on the stock market.

Mutual Insurer – a mutual insurer is an insurance company that is owned by the policyholders. A mutual company pays **dividends** to its policy owners.

Surrender - Surrender is when the policy owner decides to voluntarily take part or all the cash value from the policy. Surrendering all the cash value from the policy effectively ends the policy. Surrender charges are sometimes applicable based on when this money is taken from the policy. If surrender is done to end or terminate the policy then it becomes a taxable event. The policy owner will be charged taxes and surrender fees if applicable.

Lapse - When a policy owner decides to discontinue paying premiums and as a result terminates the policy, the policy is then lapsed. This also could cause a taxable event in a permanent life insurance policy.

Reinstatement - Reinstatement is when an insurance company allows a policy owner to reinstate a previously lapsed policy due to nonpayment of premium. At this time, all back premiums would be due and the insurance company would likely request **Evidence of Insurability** meaning a medical examination would be requested. Typically, policy owners have three years to reinstate, after a policy is lapsed.

Paramedic Exam - A paramedic exam is a medical exam done on the insured during the underwriting process, and paid for by the insurance company. During the exam, the insured's height and weight, blood pressure, and pulse are recorded, as well as blood and urine samples and sometimes oral samples are taken. The insurance company may also request additional tests if necessary.

The Attending Physician Statement (APS) – The Attending Physician Statement is a written statement given by the insured's current medical doctor, or medical facility, summarizing the insured's medical records. The report includes the insured's medical history, their lifestyle, and any pertinent information regarding the insured's current health status.

Medical Information Bureau - The Medical Information Bureau (MIB), is an organization that is owned by life insurance companies that house data on life insurance applicants over the years. The data is shared by the many members of the organization. The organization is in place to recognize conflicting information on applications versus information from the MIB. Like any consumer report, consumers have the right to request their MIB report and are entitled to one free report per year.

Risk classification - Risk classification is a premium payment class used by insurance companies to determine the premiums that will be paid by policy owners, based on the overall health of the insured. Insurance companies usually have at least three premium payment classifications, which are standard, substandard, and preferred. Standard and substandard classes are usually also broken down into non-tobacco and tobacco users. It is also commonly referred to as rating or rate class.

There are many other terms and definitions of life insurance. However, what I wanted to do here is give the terms and definitions I believe are important from a consumer perspective.

In the next chapter, I will cover policy provisions, riders, options, and exclusions that are generally found in a life insurance policy.

If you are more of a visual learner, go to the link or scan below for a video explaining most of these terms.

https://youtu.be/_b-W2AOnxh0

Chapter 6

Policy Provisions, Riders, Options, and Exclusions

In this chapter I will cover policy provisions, riders, options, and exclusions, usually found in life insurance contracts.

Provisions – Policy Provisions are terms and conditions that govern a policy. Here are some provisions you can expect to find in an insurance contract:

Owners' Rights Provision – only the policy owner has rights to the policy. The policy owner chooses the beneficiaries, chooses the insured, can borrow from or against the policy, and can transfer ownership of the policy. When transferring the policy, the policy owner could do an **absolute assign** or a **collateral assign**.

An **absolute assign** involves transferring all rights of ownership. This is permanent and the new policy owner does not have to prove insurable interest.

Collateral assignment is the transfer of partial rights and it is temporary. When choosing beneficiaries, the policy owner could choose primary and contingent beneficiaries.

- The **primary beneficiary** has the first claim to the policy upon the death of the insured and can be more than one person or entity.

- The **contingent beneficiary** is the secondary beneficiary and can claim to the death benefit if the primary dies before the insured or dies at the same time as the insured.

- An **irrevocable beneficiary**, when selected by the policy owner, cannot be changed without them giving consent to the policy owner. This is an uncommon choice since it takes away the policy owners' rights. When **minor beneficiaries** are selected, the death benefit is paid to a guardian or trustee or as determined by the court. **Minor beneficiaries** will not receive a death benefit.

Free Look Provision – The free look provision allows a policy owner to look over the policy for up to 10 days after the policy is issued and return the policy for a full refund of premiums paid.

The Grace Period Provision - the grace period provision allows a policy owner 30 or 31 days after the policy premium due date to pay the policy before the policy lapses. The death benefit is still payable if it occurs during the grace period.

The Reinstatement Clause - the reinstatement clause allows for a policy to be reinstated within three years after it lapses. At the time of reinstatement, insurable interest must be proven. All back premiums, loans, and interest are due immediately to bring the policy to its current status.

The Incontestability Clause - the incontestability clause prevents a life insurance company from denying a claim because of any statements made, or information inputted on the application, after two years as passed. Therefore, the insurance company has up to two years after the contract is issued to challenge any statements made or information entered on the application, by the insured.

The Entire Contract Clause - the entire contract clause stipulates that the policy and a copy of the application along with any riders or amendments constitute the entire contract. Any further changes would have to be agreed upon by both parties.

The Insuring Clause - the insuring clause, set forth the basic agreement between the life insurance company and the insured. It states that the insurance company promises to pay a death benefit upon the death of the insured, in exchange for the policy owner's promise to pay premiums.

Riders

Riders are additional coverages that are added on to your basic coverage for an additional fee.

Waiver of Premium Rider - the waiver of premium rider waves the premium payment if the insured becomes totally disabled. There is 6 months waiting period for this rider. After 6 months, if the insured is still disabled, all back premiums will be paid back to the policy owner. This rider expires at age 65.

Guaranteed Insurability Rider - the guaranteed insurability rider allows the policy owner to purchase additional insurance coverage without the insured, having to prove evidence of Insurability; which means that the insured would not be required to do paramedic exam. This rider specifies in the policy when additional coverage can be purchased. The rider expires at age 40, which means no additional insurance can be purchased after age 40.

Accidental Death and Dismemberment Rider - The Accidental Death and Dismemberment rider pays an additional death benefit if the insured dies in an accident. It also pays out a benefit if the insurer does not die, but was dismembered or lost a limb or dismembered a body part. The specific terms with each specific payment are spelled out in the insurance contract.

Other Insured Rider - the other insured rider allows one or more other members of the family to also be insured under the same policy. The most common form of this rider is the **child rider** in which a parent could add the child for an additional cost under the same exact policy, without having a separate policy for the child or children.

The Cost-of-Living Rider - the cost-of-living rider automatically increases the insurance coverage to address inflation.

The Accelerated Death Benefits Rider – also known as the living benefits rider makes a percentage of the death benefit available, while the insured is still alive. It is paid out if the insured is deemed chronically ill or terminally ill. **Chronic Illness** is when it is deemed that the insured cannot do two or more of the seven daily activities without assistance. A **terminal illness** is when the illness will result in the death of the insured within one or two years. Some examples of terminal illnesses are advanced cancer, dementia, lung disease, and advanced heart disease. Accelerated death benefit riders could also appear in the form of **long-term care rider.** Regardless of the title or the term it is given to any company, it all does the same thing. It makes a significant portion of the death benefit available while the insured is alive in order to help pay for major medical expenses.

Options

Policy options: policy options are broken down into three categories. They are non-forfeiture options, dividend options, and settlement options.

Non-Forfeiture Options: - Non-forfeiture options are guaranteed values, which means these are guaranteed to the policy owner and cannot be taken away. Here are the three most common non-forfeiture options.

> **Cash** - The cash option allows the policy owner to surrender the policy for the cash value that is built up in the policy. That cash value would be paid out to the policy owner minus any surrender charges or any interest or loans that are owed. After a policy is surrendered for the cash value, the insured no longer has any coverage.

> **The Reduced Paid Up Option** - The reduced paid-up option allows the policy owner to use the built-up cash value at the time of execution to purchase a paid-up permanent life insurance policy at a reduced face amount. This usually can be executed in the eighth year of the policy or after, due to the **7 pay test** in permanent life insurance policies.

Extended Term Option - This is where the policy owner could use the cash value in the policy to convert to an extended term insurance for the same face value amount.

Dividend Options:

Dividend options are found in Mutual Life Insurance companies that pay dividends to their policy owners. Unlike the non-forfeiture options, dividend options are not guaranteed. Here are the most common dividend options found in permanent life insurance policies.

Cash - the policy owner can choose to receive the dividend paid in cash directly to them. There would be no taxes paid on the receipt of dividends since the IRS codes this as a return of excess premiums paid.

Application to Reduce Premiums – With this option, the policy owner can choose to apply the dividends towards the reduction of the next year's premium.

Accumulation of Interest - This option keeps the dividends in the policy to earn additional interest. This is a very common choice, especially for policy owners who wants to maximize their policy cash value growth.

Paid up Additions - Paid up additions is when the dividend is used to purchase additional death benefit to the original policy. In today's insurance business, paid-up additions is also used as a rider, where regular premium payments can be used to pay for additional death benefit as well as to purchase more cash value, especially in permanent policies designed for high cash value upfront.

Policy Provisions, Riders, Options, and Exclusions

Paid Up Option – the paid-up option uses the dividends and interest to pay up the policy earlier.

One Year Term Option – the one-year term option, otherwise known as OYT, is when the dividends are used to purchase one-year term insurance in addition to the existing policy's face amount.

Settlement Options:

Settlement options are the various ways the death benefit proceeds are paid to the named beneficiaries. The policy owner can select this ahead of time. If no selection is made, then the lump sum payment is the default option, or the beneficiary may decide to receive it in another way. Most people are unaware that a policy owner has various settlement options. They are only familiar with the one that is most common which is the lump sum payment. However, other settlement options allow the death benefit to be paid out like an annuity. Other options include the **fixed period installment option**, the **life income option**, and the **life income with period certain option**. The fixed period installments will pay out the death benefit payment in installments to the named beneficiary for a fixed period of time. In other words, a fixed dollar amount would be paid out on a monthly, quarterly, semiannually, or annual basis, for a specified number of years. The life income option guarantees payment based on the beneficiary's life expectancy. The life income with period certain option combines the fixed period installments and the life income option in which it guarantees income for the life expectancy of the beneficiary, up to a certain minimum time.

Exclusions

While it is very important to know all the options and additions in a policy, it's also very important to know what's not included in your policy or what's excluded from your policy. Here are the most common exclusions found in life insurance policies.

Aviation - Aviation as a hobby on a non-commercial flight or any private piloting is usually excluded.

Hazardous Occupation or Hobbies - any hazardous occupations that can be life-threatening or dangerous hobbies such as bungee jumping and sky diving are generally excluded.

Suicide - Suicide is only excluded within the first two years of the policy (suicide clause). After two years, the insurance company cannot refuse to pay a death benefit because of suicide.

War and military service - typically this is excluded from a life insurance policy if an insured dies during war or as a result of an act of war or military service.

Status clause - this excludes ALL causes of death while the insured is on active duty in the military.

Results clause - only excludes benefits if the insured is killed as an act of war.

While these are all common exclusions, they must be excluded in the written contract to be recognized. If these are not written as exclusions in the policy, then the life insurance company cannot deny a death benefit as a result of any of these causes of death

You know you need life insurance but are not sure what to get or what company to buy from? Go to my calendar link below, myself or a member of my team will give you a free 30-minute consultation. Do it while it is still free!

https://www.calendbook.com/cbeckles27/lifeinsuranceconsultation

PART 2
ADVANCE STRATEGIES

Chapter 7

Policy Owners Rights

Policy ownership is such a very important aspect of life insurance that I felt the need to dedicate a chapter to it. I believe the leverage and control that you get from owning a life insurance policy is one of the best-kept secrets in the financial services industry.

In this chapter, I will describe some of the main policy owners' rights and explain how individuals and businesses can take advantage of them and use these rights to their benefit. The first right that I want to discuss is the right to choose a beneficiary. This right allows the policy owner to select who will receive the death benefit when the insured dies. This right gives the policy owner a lot of power, leverage, and control. What is also great is that the policy owner can change beneficiaries any time they want. Whenever they change beneficiary, insurable interest does not have to be proven. Insurable interest only needs to be proven at application which means there no longer must be proof that the new beneficiary or beneficiaries will experience a financial loss when the insured dies. This type of power and control could come in very handy in many circumstances. For example, a married couple that had insurance on each other and then gets divorced, they may want to change beneficiaries after the divorce. The policy owner could change the beneficiary since they are no longer married. Just to be clear, it does not require something like this to happen for a policy owner to change his or her beneficiary. A policy owner can change beneficiaries at any time, for any reason; no questions asked! Also, in a case where the policy owner wanted a minor as their beneficiary, they can elect an adult to act as temporary trustee and change the beneficiary when the minor becomes of age. Death benefit proceeds cannot be paid out to minors.

The policy owner can also choose the insured. As mentioned earlier, the insured and the policy owner are the same person, in most cases. However, not always, the policy owner is sometimes a **third-party owner**. So, in the case where the policy owner is not the insured, they can choose whoever they want the insured to be. **Insurable Interest** must be proven at this time of application. Since insurable interest must be proven, the policy owner will have to show that there's a relationship between them and the insured as well as prove that the beneficiary will suffer a financial loss when the insured dies.

Typically, third-party ownership happens in a case where there's a spouse or family member. For example, a husband may have his wife as an insured and he is the policy owner and is paying for the policy. Or he may have his children as the insured, and he is the policy owner and paying for the policy. This is also a good strategy in a case where the policy owner does not qualify to be insured, but still wants to take advantage of the policy owners' benefits. In this case, the policy owner would have insurance on their healthy spouse, and then they would be the owner and would be able to do the things that policy owners do. For example, an ownership right like borrowing against the policy. That takes us to the next right that I want to discuss, which is policy loans.

The policy owner has the right to borrow against the policy's **cash value**. This only applies to permanent life insurance policies. Once a policy owner has built up enough cash value in their policy, they can borrow against the policy to do whatever they want. It also gives them the flexibility to pay back that policy loan whenever they want to. This flexibility is possible because any outstanding loan is collateralized by the death benefit. If an insured dies with an outstanding policy loan, the loan balance with interest would be subtracted from the death benefit before it is paid to the beneficiary.

Scan QR code or Go to the following link to watch a short video where I explain the above example

https://youtu.be/VQ_gC-MpsoI

Policy owners can also transfer ownership of the policy. For example, if a parent bought the policy on their child as the insured when the child becomes an adult, they may choose to transfer the ownership of the policy into the child's name. However, there would be a tax consequence on any interest earned during the policy up to that point. Another good example of policy owner transfer is of the transfer of ownership from a person to an entity. For example, a policy owner might transfer the ownership from themselves as an individual to a trust. As people grow with their policies, they often learn different strategies that allows them to make their policy function better or work for them better in the long run. This is why it is so great that policy ownership provides you with a lot of flexibility, leverage, and control. Sometimes people are also not initially set up in the position they want to be, but they do not want to wait to get life insurance. Therefore, they make changes as their circumstances change, and their goals and dreams become a reality.

As mentioned in the previous chapter policy owners also have rights to non-forfeiture options which they cannot lose and cannot be taken away from them. The policy owner may have a premium payment schedule to be paid for the rest of their life. However, they change their mind later and want to stop paying premiums. They have the right to exercise, the reduced paid-up option, and stop paying premiums completely! Many people do not know that whole life insurance provides this flexibility.

And of course, policy owners have the right to settlement options. They can cancel the policy whenever they want for the cash value and they can decide how the death benefit proceeds will be distributed. The main takeaway I want you to get from this chapter is that as a policy owner in a life insurance policy, especially a permanent life insurance policy, it gives you a lot of flexibility, leverage, and control that does not exist in other financial vehicles. Other financial vehicles tend to have a lot of risks, a lot of restrictions, a lot of limitations, and not a lot of control. Life Insurance ownership is still one of the world's best-kept secrets!

Chapter 8

Cash Value & Policy Loans

Cash Value - I purposely did not include cash value in the definition section earlier in chapter 5, because it is a very important component of a permanent life insurance policy. I wanted to explain it in detail.

So, what is the cash value of a permanent life insurance contract? The cash value of a life insurance policy is a savings account within the policy. The cash value is made up of premiums paid, interest earned, as well as dividends paid, in some instances. A permanent life insurance policy has two premium buckets when you pay your premium. One bucket is the cost of insurance bucket, which has the cost for the death benefit, the cost for the agent commission, and insurance fees. The second bucket is the cash value savings bucket. Based on the way your policy is structured and designed, it will determine how much of your premium goes to the cost of insurance bucket and how much of your premium goes to the cash value bucket. See illustrations below.

Get Your L.I.F.E. Together

Figure 1A

Cost of Insurance Bucket

Figure 1B

Savings Account Bucket

Base Premium	**Cash Value/Paid Up Addition**
Insurance Cost (Death Benefit)	No Cash value start of policy
Administrative cost	No paid up Additions
Agent commission	No Supplemental term insurance

Cash Value & Policy Loans

Figure 2A	Figure 2B
Cost of Insurance Bucket	**Savings Account Bucket**

Base Premium	**Cash Value/Paid Up Addition**
Insurance Cost (Minimum Death Benefit)	Maximum Cash value
Low administrative cost	Paid up additional insurance and cash value
Very low agent commission	Supplemental term insurance

As you can see in the first diagram, all the premium paid is going into the cost of insurance bucket. Therefore, it has a higher death benefit. Initially, none of the premium is going into the cash value bucket at the start of the policy. Therefore, it takes a while to build up cash value. This is the basic structure found in most permanent life insurance policies. It is front loaded with the insurance costs. In the second diagram, most of the initial cash is going into the cash value bucket. Most of the premiums paid is going into the cash value bucket and less into the cost of insurance bucket therefore, it is a lower death benefit, and the cash value is maximized. Though the cash value safely grows interest, it is important not to compare or consider it an investment. An investment involves high risk, your account value could go up or down, and you can lose your principal. Cash value life insurance, however, should be compared more to a bank account. Therefore, I would compare it to a savings account in a bank. A cash value earns interest that is paid by the insurance company from their general account or based on the performance of an index when it is tied to an index in an IUL. Dividend payments can also be added to a cash value bucket to maximize the growth of the cash value; if the policy owner chooses to do that when the policy is with a mutual insurance company that pays out dividends. Cash value plays a very important role in a permanent life insurance policy. It can be used for policy loans, it can be used for automatic premium loans, used for premium offset, reduce paid-up, or for it can be surrendered for cash.

Since I will take a deeper dive into policy loans later in the chapter, let us discuss the other uses.

Annual premium loan comes in the form of a rider in many policies. You usually do not have to pay a fee for it upfront. However, you are charged a fee if you did have to use it. What it does is allow you to take a loan from the cash value in your policy to pay your premium if you get into a situation where you were not able to pay your premium. This way the policy can continue to go on without lapsing. A premium offset is when the policy is set up to stop paying out of pocket premiums after a certain number of years, and the policy's cash value pays the minimum premium; otherwise known as the base premium. The policy owner no longer pays out of pocket premium payments to keep their policy going. Instead, the cash value will pay the base premium until the insured dies, or until the policy expires. The reduced paid up option using the cash value is when, after a certain number of years, not earlier than the eighth year, the policy owner could exercise it to completely stop paying premiums.

Here is how it works.

After the cash value has been built up in the policy for a number of years, it's used as a single payment to buy a reduced amount of permanent life insurance coverage. The cash value will also reduce in value after it is used to purchase paid-up life insurance. Absolutely no additional premiums will be paid after that. The policy owner cannot pay any additional premium after the reduced paid-up option has been exercised with the cash value. The policy, however, will continue to grow interest, as well as increase in death benefit, as the cash continues to grow. Hopefully that all made sense to you. In essence, the cash value is the monetary value of the life insurance policy. Therefore, the policy owner also has the ability to surrender the cash value for a cash payment and end the policy.

Policy Loans - Policy loans go hand in hand with a cash value because as mentioned before, the cash value is what you would use to borrow against when taking out a policy loan. The policy owner could take up to the amount of cash value that is available in the policy and will pay back the loan, with interest, based on terms spelled out in the contract. The interest can be a fixed rate or a variable rate; again, based on the terms of the contract. The policy owner may choose to pay back the loan when they want to. They can also choose to pay back just the interest or they could pay back the interest and the loan amount at the same time. There is a lot of flexibility when paying back a policy loan. The policy owner may choose to pay it back in one shot, in monthly payments, quarterly, semiannually, or in any way they choose to. The insurance company does not care when a policy owner pays it back. This is because policy loans are collateralized by the policy's death benefit. Should the insured die, and there is an outstanding loan balance, the loan balance, as well as interest owed, will be subtracted from the death benefit before payment. Please keep in mind that it is not a great practice to not pay back policy loan in a timely manner, because the cash value will have to borrow from itself to pay at least the interest; if the loan is not being paid back.

At minimum, the policy owner should pay the loan interest out of pocket. If a policy loan is not paid back for a long period of time, and the cash value is not strong enough to support the policy, it can lapse; so please beware. This is an aspect that is usually not shared when people talk about life insurance especially on social media. A great benefit to policy loans in a life insurance policy is that there are very little limitations or restrictions. You can borrow against your policy for whatever you want, whenever you want, for as often as you can. You can access your cash value for emergency funds, for your children's education, for a family wedding or any life event, to buy your personal home, or to use as working capital for your business. Whatever your need may be, a cash value life insurance policy is a great place to store your cash for liquid access, while taking advantage of the tax benefit of loans.

Chapter 9

Tax Advantages of Life Insurance

First, I want to start this chapter by saying I am not a CPA. I am not a tax attorney, nor am I a tax professional. The purpose of this chapter is to discuss specific tax laws and codes as they relate to life insurance. If you are unclear about anything that is discussed here, you may also seek the counsel or consultation of a tax professional.

Before I get into the IRS codes that are important to life insurance, I want to give you some background history on why they come about and why they are important. It was about 1979 or 1980 when EF Hutton, the man credited with introducing Universal Life, brought this new product to the market. Universal Life differs from whole life because it provides flexibility in premium and flexibility in death benefit. Due to this flexibility, what policy owners were doing was putting in as much premium as possible for the least amount of death benefit in their universal life policies. In essence, what they were doing was self-insuring themselves while taking advantage of the high-interest environment at the time. As a result, heavily funding their policies while taking the least amount of death benefit, policy owners were gaining double digit returns on the cash value of their policies, with no risk to the insurance company. This caused the IRS to step in and get Congress to create new laws and implement new regulations to the life insurance industry. For life insurance to be considered life insurance, the insurer, which is the life insurance company, must be at risk for a death benefit. Therefore, self-insurance was not permitted, and if a life insurance policy violates these new laws, it will no longer be treated as standard life insurance policy.

If you go to the IRS website or perhaps do a Google search about the codes that regulates life insurance, you will find that it is very complicated and difficult to understand, even for myself. What I will do here is attempt to make it as simple as possible for you and focus on what is most important for you to know. Here we go!

The three main IRS tax codes that regulates how cash value life insurance works are IRS tax code 7702, IRS tax code 72e, and IRS tax code 101a. The three main laws that updated what these codes are today are the Tax and Fiscal Responsibility Act of 1982, otherwise known as TEFRA, the Deficit Reduction Act of 1984, otherwise known as DEFRA, and the Technical and Miscellaneous Revenue Act of 1988, otherwise known as TAMRA. In 1982, Congress passed TEFRA into law. It was passed to cut the budget deficit through federal spending cuts, tax increases, and take reform measures. As a result of this legislation, Congress reversed some elements of the Economic Recovery Tax Act of 1981(ERTA). It modified the tax advantages of life insurance contracts so that policy owners could not abuse the advantages and use their policies like an investment anymore.

This regulated the practice of using life insurance policies as an investment vehicle to make very high returns without paying any taxes. Congress passed DEFRA in 1984 to fill some gaps that TEFRA failed to address. In other words, they did not fully get it right. Therefore, DEFRA had to be put in place to redefine and control the abuse of using life insurance contracts as an investment, masked as life insurance. TAMRA was passed in 1988 to update section 72e of the IRS code. It added the 7-pay test to whole life insurance policies. The 7-pay test basically states that the total premiums paid within the first seven years of a whole life policy cannot exceed the total amount that will be needed to fully pay up the policy within those seven years. If the 7-pay test is violated in a whole life policy, then the policy becomes a Modified Endowment Contract, also known as a MEC, and causes a permanent life insurance policy to lose the tax advantages. Specifically, a policy that is considered a MEC would cause a taxable event if the policy owner accesses the cash value in any form.

Once TEFRA and DEFRA were passed, there were two tests that a permanent life insurance, sometimes called a cash value life insurance policy, had to pass. These tests were updated as now part of section 7702. The first is the Cash Value Accumulation Test (CVAT). The CVAT states that the cash surrender value, basically the total cash value, of a contract may not at any time exceed the net single premium, which would have to be paid at such time to fund any future death benefit under the contract. That means the total cash value cannot be more than what it will cost to purchase any future paid up death benefit with a single premium payment. The life insurance policy must pass this test throughout the entire existence of the policy. Life insurance companies are usually very good about making policy owners aware of when they are in danger of going over this limit. It is also to a policy owner's advantage to have an agent or broker that will help them monitor this.

The next test that needs to be passed under code 7702 is the Guideline Premium and Corridor Test (GPCT), sometimes referred to as the Guideline Single Premium (GSP). The Guideline Premium and Corridor Test requires that the sum of the total premiums paid under a permanent life insurance contract does not at any time exceed the guideline premium limitation at such time. In other words, the policy owner cannot have paid more premium into the policy than would be necessary to fund any future death benefit. Just to put some clarity on these tests, the 7-pay test in a whole life policy is testing the premiums paid within the first seven years. The Guideline Premium and Corridor Test is testing the premium payment throughout the entire contract. The Cash Value Accumulation Test is testing the total cash value throughout the entire contract, which includes premiums paid, interest credited, as well as dividends paid into the policy which makes up the entire cash value. Once TEFRA and DEFRA updated code 7702, here are some key bullet points to takeaway:

- IRS code 7702 is used to determine a legit life insurance contract.

- It stipulates that certain permanent life insurance contract builds cash value over time. These types of permanent life insurance include whole life, universal Life, and variable life contracts.

- Code 7702 is used to differentiate between income from a genuine life insurance product, and income from an investment vehicle.

- It stipulates that the proceeds of a true life insurance contract receive favorable tax treatments.

- It stipulates that the proceeds, meaning the cash value gains, of a contract that does not meet the IRS definition of life insurance, are taxed as ordinary income.

- It stipulates that if an insurance policy fails section 7702 criteria, then it becomes a modified endowment contract and permanently loses its tax advantaged status.

In summary, section 7702, section 72e, and section 101a of the IRS tax code allows the policy owner to grow their policy tax free, access their policy tax free, and transfer the death benefit to their policy tax free, as long as these codes are adhered to. If any of the three tests mentioned are violated, then the policy will become a Modified Endowment Contract (MEC). When a permanent life insurance contract becomes a MEC status, then the policy owner permanently cannot access the policy nor grow interest on the policy without tax consequences. However, a MEC policy can still be transferred to the named beneficiary tax free.

Hopefully, you now have a good understanding of the tax advantages of life insurance, and how these laws and IRS codes pertain to it. Now it is time to learn how you can use life insurance as leverage to build wealth, and provide retirement income.

There are 3 times when a taxable event can occur within a life insurance policy. Go to the link or scan OR code below to see these 3 taxable events discussed.

Get Your L.I.F.E. Together

https://youtu.be/jgexzxsAw4o

Chapter 10

The Infinite Banking Concept

The first thing I want to make clear to you is that infinite banking is not a product. You cannot buy a product called Infinite Banking. So, if infinite banking is not a product and you cannot purchase it then what is infinite banking? I am glad you ask.

Infinite Banking is a concept in which you leverage the cash in a cash value life insurance policy to borrow against and use it repeatedly until the policy matures. Essentially what you are doing is you are using the cash value in your life insurance policy to replace the bank. So, instead of going to the bank for a loan, for whatever reason, whether it is for personal or business reasons, you would replace that normal procedure of borrowing from the bank with borrowing against the cash value in your life insurance policy. If the Infinite Banking concept is about leverage, then why is it always associated with life insurance? It's associated with life insurance because only life insurance allows you to have this type of leverage and control. Other financial vehicles do not give you the leverage and control that you get with being a policy owner with a life insurance policy.

The two main components of the Infinite Banking strategy are the cash value and policy loans. Since we already covered them in an earlier chapter, I will not spend much time going over those concepts or those components. Instead, I will give you practical scenarios in which you can utilize this concept with these components to achieve your financial goals. There are many ways in which you can utilize this concept. You can use it to purchase your regular everyday things and pay your bills. You can use this concept to pay for major purchases. You can use it to pay for major life changes such as a wedding in the family, or such as paying for your children's education. You can use this concept as working capital for your business as well as using it for investments in real estate or in any other investment. My recommendation would be that you use this strategy to purchase assets that produce cash flow, or use it to invest in your business, or make investments that are going to give you back a return. In other words, use it to purchase assets that makes you money, and not liabilities that takes money away from you.

Now that you have an understanding of the concept and what it can be used for, let's now talk about how it actually works. The first thing I want you to understand is that the policy has to be designed correctly to operate in this manner. Reason being, the focus of this policy is to produce maximum cash value so you can borrow against that policy as early as possible. The typical policy that is not structured specifically for infinite banking takes a while to build up cash value. Usually the first year or two, there is no cash value to use when you are paying your premium. This is because the basic policy is structured for maximum death benefit upfront. A policy designed specifically for infinite banking is structured minimizing the death benefit initially and maximizing the cash value so that you can immediately access the cash value if you wanted to.

A key element of this strategy is that when you borrow against your cash value, your full cash value continues to earn interest. Meanwhile, you borrow against it to use for whatever you want or need, especially to purchase assets. What this gives you is no lost opportunity cost which means you have uninterrupted growth on your entire cash value, meanwhile, you use it as leverage to borrow from the insurance company. It's basically having your dollars work in two places at the same time. It is important to also note that once you have cash value built up in your life insurance policy, by contract, the life insurance company must lend you the money if you want to borrow, up to the amount of cash value you have in the policy. There is no credit check needed. There is no application needed. It is simply a request made by the policy owner to access cash from the insurance company based on the amount of cash value that the policy owner has. This is the type of leverage and control a policy owner has. That is not available in other financial vehicles. Once the policy owner borrows against their cash value, they would pay back the amount they borrowed plus interest if paid after a year. Once the policy owner pays back the loan with interest, they can now borrow against that policy for the full amount once more, and they can do that over and over and over and over again. Hence, the "infinite" in the term infinite banking. For example, let us say a policy owner has $100,000 of cash value available and they wanted to borrow against 80,000 of that. They will remain with 20,000 cash in cash value. Let's say the loan interest is 5%, and the policy owner is going to pay that back in full the following year. This means that the policy owner will owe $80,000 plus the 5% of the $80,000 loan which is $4,000 for a total of $84,000 payment. Let us also assume that the interest being earned on the cash value is 5%, the interest being earned would be 5% on top of the $100,000. The loan will be paid back for $84,000 and then the new cash value will be $105,000. Since 5% was added on to the entire $100,000, not just on $20,000 of the cash value in the policy.

This brings me to direct recognition and indirect recognition. Many people are confused as to what direct recognition and indirect recognition is. They think it means if interest is credited or not credited when you borrow a loan against your policy. This is not what it means at all. It simply means that the interest of the borrowed funds is recognized by the insurance company when it is direct recognition, and the funds that are borrowed in an indirect recognition company are not recognized and treated all the same. In other words, in both cases, a policy owner is getting credit on the entire cash value, including borrowed funds. That is the amount that is borrowed against as well as the amount that's not borrowed against. They are just treated and credited differently in a direct recognition company. However, in an indirect recognition company, they are all credited the same. Let me give an example to make it a little clearer.

Let us say a policy owner has $100,000 of cash value and they borrowed $70,000. Let us also assume that the interest rate is 6% on the loan. And let us assume that the credit that they are getting for interest is 5%. A company that is a direct recognition company may want to adjust their normal 5% interest credit on the borrowed portion ($70.000) to 6% to not penalize the policy owner for borrowing against their policy. In other words, they do not want to credit the policy owner 5% on the $70,000 and 5% credit on the remaining $30,000 in the policy. This way they pay 6% for the loan, get 6% interest credit for the $70,000, and 5% interest credit on the remaining $30,000. Again, simply recognizing that $70,000 was borrowed and treating that $70,000 differently from the remaining 30,000 of cash value that was left in the policy. In an indirect recognition company. The entire $100,000, that is the $70,000 that is borrowed and the $30,000 that is remaining of cash value would get the same 5% interest credit. So again, to hammer home the point, direct recognition just means that the insurance company recognizes the amount that was borrowed against the policy up against the cash value and treats the crediting of that amount differently from the remaining cash value that is left; and in an indirect recognition it does not recognize the amount that was borrowed against, and treat the entire cash value all the same, and credited all as one. Hopefully, that makes sense to you.

The next attractive aspect of policy loans is loan arbitrage. Arbitrage occurs when the interest rate you are credited on your cash value is a higher interest rate than the loan interest rate when you borrowed against, your policy. Let us use the $100,000 as an example again. Let us say the interest credited on $100,000 for a particular year is 8% which means the new cash value will be $108,000. Let us say the policy owner borrowed against the entire 100,000 at a 5% interest rate means the policy owner will pay back $105,000. Therefore, the policy owner had a 3% arbitrage. They were credited $8,000 on their 100,000. However, they only paid $5,000 for borrowing that $100,000. The concept of arbitrage is usually found in policies that are tied to the stock market such as IULs or policies that are invested in the stock market, such as VULs. Now that you understand the concept of infinite banking and how it works, let us now look at how policy owners have used it to start, grow, and maintain their businesses.

If you watch the movie, The Founder, which is the story about the history of the McDonald's Corporation. You will see how Ray Kroc actually did whatever it took to keep his business going. He even got himself in so much debt to keep his business afloat. What you may not have known is that Ray Kroc borrowed against his whole life insurance policies to use as working capital for his business. Even though the concept of infinite banking was not born yet, what Ray Kroc was doing is like what we do today. He was able to borrow against his whole life policy for operational costs in his business, such as paying his employees. Even though this was not the only strategy he used to keep his business going, we can all say that this has contributed to accomplishing his goals. Today McDonald's have served billions of customers worldwide, and is the second largest restaurant food chain in the entire world. Another famous entrepreneur that utilizes a whole life policy for his business is Walt Disney. Walt had a dream and a vision that no one else could see, but him. He went to several banks for financing and they all turned him down, because no one believed in his ideas nor his creation. No one believed that these characters that he created could become a success. Thankfully, he had liquid access to his whole life policy, where he was able to borrow against his whole life policy to start Disney World. Think about that for a second. Disney as we know it today, would probably not have existed if Walt Disney did not believe in himself enough to move forward despite being turned down by so many banks. There may not have been a Magic Kingdom, a Mickey Mouse, a Donald Duck, nor anything Disney at all; had not he bank on himself by borrowing against his whole life policy to start his company.

J.C. Penney is another entrepreneur that utilizes the cash value in his whole life policy to continue his business during the late 1920s when the stock market crashed and many banks were failing and going out of business. The Great Depression followed and J. C. Penney did not have many options besides his life insurance policy. Due to the safe and secure and conservative way of investing, life insurance companies were able to withstand the tough economic times. And were one of the few ways to get access to capital since many financial institutions were failing. Though most likely JC Penney had his whole life policy, mainly because of the death benefit, luckily, at this time, he had built up enough cash value where he was able to borrow against his policy to get his business through some of the toughest economic times in American history.

Other well-known major corporations such as Starbucks, Coca Cola, Pfizer, and many others, utilize corporate owned life insurance(COLI) to store working capital for their business. They can do this by putting life insurance on major key employees who is employed by their corporation mainly executives. Since the company could suffer a financial loss if an executive dies while working for the company. This proves insurable interest. Not only are the companies financially protected if the employee dies they also have that money to store as capital while safely earning a good return. The executive or employee also benefits by getting compensated if they work for the company for a certain number of years. Their family also usually gets a portion of the death benefit. This is an incentive to allow the company to take out a policy on them. Many major banks also own billions of dollars in permanent life insurance. Their main purpose is to have a strong asset on their balance sheet since the Federal Reserve requires banks to have a certain percentage of cash in reserves. This category is called tier-one assets, which are assets that are safe and liquid in case of unexpected demand. Banks usually put 30 to 40% of this tier-one asset category in permanent life insurance policies. Not only does this show up as a strong asset on their balance sheet, but the death benefit is usually used for employee programs such as pensions and other employee compensation programs. So, you've seen how major corporations and banks have utilized these strategies, as well as very successful entrepreneurs. Now, let us look at how any individual such as yourself could utilize this strategy to help build their finances long term.

Real estate is a great place to use this strategy. Real Estate Investors also understand this concept because it is like what some of them do. What I mean by that is they understand the strategy of leverage. For example, if a person bought a property that has equity in it, like a flip property that was bought and renovated and now has more value than what the investor invested in it. That investor could leverage that property by taking out a line of credit against that property to go purchase another property while still making money on the first property in the form of rental income. Now the investor would be making money on both properties. It is like borrowing against your life insurance policy. Your money in your policy continues to grow uninterruptedly, meanwhile you use the insurance company's money to purchase income producing assets and investments. This is why many real estate investors understand the concept and utilize it in their businesses.

Okay, so let us look at an example. Let us say a real estate investor is purchasing a property all in for $350,000. This means that the purchase price of the property, plus whatever funds is needed to repair the property and get it in retail market condition is $350,000 all in. Let us say that the investor needs to bring in $50,000 to the closing table to acquire the property, which includes closing costs. The investor could borrow $50,000 against their permanent life insurance policy and then utilize either the bank or a hard money lender to fund the rest of the deal. Now let us say that the same property is worth $500,000 when fixed up. That investor could sell that property for 500,000 minus any closing costs, pay back the loan owed, and payback the $50,000 borrowed from their permanent life insurance policy, with interest, and still walk away with a strong five-figure profit. In this scenario, their life insurance policy will continue to earn the interest on the entire amount they earn after walking away from the real estate deal with profits. This investor now has more cash value to borrow against to do it repeatedly, and eventually can use their life insurance policy to fund an entire deal. This is truly a win, win situation!

Another example will be to use it for trucking. Imagine you have $100,000 of cash value built up in your policy and you wanted to buy two trucks at $25,000 each. You can borrow against your policy for $60,000 to buy the trucks and get your business started. Imagine those two trucks produces you a total of $20,000 in income per month. In no time you would be able to pay back your insurance policy for the cost of that truck in less than a year. You would be able to pay back the insurance policy for the cost of the truck and the cost of running the business; then you would be making huge profits from there. Again, your $100,000 will continue to grow interest as if you never borrowed against it; another win, win situation!

The rental car business is another vehicle that you can use your life insurance policy to use as leverage. Think for a minute that you have $100,000 of cash value in your policy, and you wanted to get $50,000 to buy five used cars to rent out. Let us say that each car produces $1,000 per month in income. That will be $5,000 per month. In one year, you could most likely pay back that loan that you borrowed from your policy. After the cars are paid off, your expenses will reduce to the cost of insurance and maintenance, therefore increasing your profit margin. There are many other ways to utilize this strategy as a way of leveraging your cash to purchase income producing assets that will generate income to pay back the loan and put profits in your pocket, meanwhile still earning interest on your original cash value simultaneously. Those that are most familiar with the Infinite Banking strategy, as explained by Nelson Nash, the man credited with creating this strategy. It gives you the freedom to utilize and leverage your cash value in your life insurance policy to do everything in your life. This Includes purchasing liabilities such as your own car that you drive, paying your credit card bills, etc.

If you have a good strategy and the numbers work out for you, then by all means you can use it for that as well. It gives you a level of control and freedom to do whatever you want with it. However, my personal recommendation is that you only use it to purchase income producing assets, simply because you are now not liable to paying this back yourself. The income generated from the assets you use the loan to purchase, will pay the loan back. In any case, if things do not work out as planned, you still have the option in your back pocket to be able to pay the loan back later if you want, or not pay it at all, and have your death benefit pay it. Bottom line is, the infinite banking strategy gives you that leverage to have your dollars working in two places at the same time while helping you to build wealth in the insurance policy as well building more wealth with your policy loans. Using this strategy correctly and effectively could help you build up tremendous long-term wealth. Since this strategy allows you to rinse and repeat, the possibilities are endless! If the banks and the corporations are using this strategy to help run their business and earn more cash safely, why shouldn't you? A common mistake most individuals make is to think that they must have a lot of money to get started. This strategy is not only for the rich. The key is to start at your level. You do not need to have the money like the banks do in order to have a policy like this. Start at your level and build as you go. You can add another policy or policies as your income grows.

To learn more about this tremendous strategy, visit the URLs below or scan QR code.

https://youtu.be/lv6y1VkfbCk

Get Your L.I.F.E. Together

https://youtu.be/08E3eNnqsr8

Chapter 11

Using Life Insurance for Retirement Income

Usually when people think about retirement income, they do not think about using life insurance as a vehicle for retirement income. Typically, people are using traditional methods such as 401K, or IRAs. However, there are some fundamental issues with using those vehicles for retirement. They are not as great of a retirement vehicle as advertised. Just think about it; when people think of having money for retirement income, what are typically their main concerns? People are usually concerned whether they do have enough money saved up for retirement. They also want to make sure that it is safe and they do not lose money. In a recent study done by Allianz Life Insurance Company of North America, a survey that was taken by on middle age Americans which is between 30 and 45 years old. Here are the results in terms of what their concerns were; 59% of them worry that inflation will prevent them from enjoying the retirement they were thinking of having. 52% of them do not think that they have enough money saved up for retirement, and 49% of them want to keep their tax bill as low as possible. Taxes is a major concern for people planning for retirement as well. If these things are what people are mainly concerned about, then obviously, an IRA or 401K will not be the right solution for them.

The first issue with an IRA or 401K is that there are too many restrictions. It is really. If you really look at it; even though the account is under an individual's name. The individual does not really own it, it's for their benefit, but they don't have the control to do what they need to do with it. There it is limited as to how much they can put into the program. And it is also limited on when they can access it so therefore it's not liquid. If any rules are violated there is a penalty. Usually, an individual cannot access their 401K or their IRA account before they are 59 ½. If so, there will be an IRS penalty of 10% as well as taxes charged. You are also limited as to how much you can put into the account.

As of 2023, the limit an individual could put into an IRA is $6,500 per year or $7,500 per year, if they are over 50 years old. Not only are there limitations as to how much you can put in it, there are limitations has to when you can access the funds. Even though 401k does give you a larger limit, it still has limitations based on your different categories.

The overall limitation though the total amount anyone could put in a 401 K as of 2023 is $66,000 and $73,500, including catch up contributions according to the IRS. The next issue with these vehicles is that they are usually tied to the stock market. And as we know with the stock market you can earn money, and you can also lose. This is usually a strategy for someone that can afford to lose during a particular period. This is not a good strategy for retirement income;

retirement income should be safe and secure. The last thing a person need to worry about is losing some of their retirement income. This is why many individuals panic and do not get the returned that the market could give over a longer period. People get emotionally tied to their money once they see themselves losing, they automatically panic and sell their stocks. Then once they see things getting back, good again, they buy. They are doing the opposite of what you should be doing when you are invested in the stock market. They are selling while they are in a down position. And they are buying when the stock is rising again, giving them comfort that the stock is doing well. So, they never get to experience the overall gains that they could have because of their emotional ties to their money, which is 100% understandable.

The next problem with these vehicles for retirement is the taxes, as illustrated earlier. People are concerned about taxes eating away their retirement income. If I asked adults in America what are their feelings about taxes within the next ten years, what do you think 9 of 10 of them would say? Do they feel that taxes will be higher in the long run? Or would it be lowered in the future? 9 out of 10 people will answer me that they believe that taxes will be higher. If this is the case, then why keep their money in a tax deferred vehicle. If taxes are going to be more in the long run, that means you will pay more later. It is going to take more from your savings.

The fact that people will keep their money, in vehicles like IRAs and 401 K's, feeling that tax will be higher in the future is crazy to me. Perhaps the reason why people still do this is because they have been sold on the idea that these are the vehicles for retirement. So, not only can people not access their money when they want to. It is also not safe due to market volatility. They usually do not get to realize the type of growth that they could have achieved long term, because of their emotions about the ups and downs of the stock market. Then they must pay taxes when they finally take their money out. All these factors result in lower retirement income; eating away your hard-earned money.

Now let us look at how life insurance can solve all these issues. First, you have liquidity. You can access your money in your cash value life insurance policy whenever you want, for whatever you want, without penalty. This is as long as you follow the IRS guidelines. What I mean by that is, you use a loan to access your money then you do not pay taxes on that money, and you do not pay a penalty nor surrender charge. Your money, in your cash value life insurance policy is also safe. When you put your money in the right policy, it is not invested in the market; therefore, it is not affected by the market volatility. You only gain interest on your cash value, you do not lose anything.

The next concern is inflation. As inflation becomes more of a problem, many people saving for retirement are worried about their dollars having a lot less value in their later years. This is why a good rate of return is necessary. A rate that will outpace inflation. The right life insurance policy will solve this problem as well. This is why many banks utilize life insurance policies as a safe way to earn a good rate of return, outpacing inflation.

Life insurance also solves the major concern of taxes. Life insurance policies are tax advantaged, if it is structured correctly, used correctly, and IRS guidelines are followed. You can access your cash through loans tax free, you grow interest on your cash value tax free, and your death benefit will pass on to your beneficiary tax free! Therefore, all your interest earned would not be eaten away by 33% or more, due to taxes. This makes a huge difference in the amount of spendable income you would have in your retirement years. So, if these traditional retirement vehicles put people at risk for losing at least a third of your final retirement income due to taxes, and they risk losing a good portion of their retirement income because of market volatility, then why do people continue to put their money there? That is a great question. The reality is most human beings do not take control of their own personal finance. They either do what they are told, give it to someone else to do, or they follow what everyone else is doing. The truth of the matter is most financial advisors, planners and consultants are told to push these types of products to the public. Therefore, as I mentioned, most people will do as they are told, or just follow what everyone else is doing. If you look at the situation truthfully, you can see that you are not the owner of any of these types of financial vehicles. You are in a partnership with the IRS. The government is the owner, because they control and determine how the vehicle is to be used, and what you can and what you cannot do. You are the beneficiary of such a vehicle, not the owner. However, with a life insurance policy, it spells out clearly in the contract that you are the owner of the contract. The insurance company is the administrator. They are responsible for managing the funds accurately, efficiently, and safely. You as a policy owner have rights to access those funds, whenever you want, for whatever you want; you are in total control!

Now just to be clear, I am not saying that investing in the stock market is bad and paying taxes is bad. All I am saying is that these types of strategies are not good for saving for retirement. The products that are advertised as good for retirement are invested in the stock market and have high tax liability which is contrary to the goal of having as much money as possible for retirement. Now to solidify this point I will show you an example of a side-by-side comparison of a 30-year-old man making $100,000 per year funding his retirement savings vehicle with $10,000 per year for 35 years, with an average interest credit of 6.6% per year. Figure 1 shows how the scenario looks if the money is invested in a traditional retirement savings account such as an IRA or 401K, with retirement income distribution beginning in year 36, at age 66. Figure 2 shows how the scenario would look if the funds were placed in an index universal life policy with income distribution also beginning in year 36, at age 66. Let us have some fun!

Figure 1

Age	Contribution	Interest	Balance	Income Distribution	After tax $
31	$10,000	6.6%	$10,660		
32	$10,000	6.6%	$22,024		
33	$10,000	6.6%	$34,137		
34	$10,000	6.6%	$47,050		
35	$10,000	6.6%	$60,815		
36	$10,000	6.6%	$75,489		
37	$10,000	6.6%	$91,132		
38	$10,000	6.6%	$107,806		
39	$10,000	6.6%	$125,581		
40	$10,000	6.6%	$144,530		
41	$10,000	6.6%	$164,729		
42	$10,000	6.6%	$186,261		
43	$10,000	6.6%	$209,214		
44	$10,000	6.6%	$233,683		
45	$10,000	6.6%	$259,765		
46	$10,000	6.6%	$287,570		
47	$10,000	6.6%	$317,209		
48	$10,000	6.6%	$348,805		
49	$10,000	6.6%	$382,486		
50	$10,000	6.6%	$418,391		
51	$10,000	6.6%	$456,664		
52	$10,000	6.6%	$497,464		
53	$10,000	6.6%	$540,957		
54	$10,000	6.6%	$587,320		
55	$10,000	6.6%	$636,743		
56	$10,000	6.6%	$689,429		
57	$10,000	6.6%	$745,590		

Age	Contribution	Rate	Value		
58	$10,000	6.6%	$805,590		
59	$10,000	6.6%	$869,419		
60	$10,000	6.6%	$937,461		
61	$10,000	6.6%	$1,009,993		
62	$10,000	6.6%	$1,087,312		
63	$10,000	6.6%	$1,169,736		
64	$10,000	6.6%	$1,257,598		
65	$10,000	6.6%	$1,351,260		
66			$1,251,260	$100,000	$67,000
67			$1,151,260	$100,000	$67,000
68			$1,051,260	$100,000	$67,000
69			$951,260	$100,000	$67,000
70			$851,260	$100,000	$67,000
71			$751,260	$100,000	$67,000
72			$651,260	$100,000	$67,000
73			$551,260	$100,000	$67,000
74			$451,260	$100,000	$67,000
75			$351,260	$100,000	$67,000
76			$251,260	$100,000	$67,000
77			$151,260	$100,000	$67,000
78			$51,260	$51,260	$34,344
79					
80					
81					
82					
83					
84					
85					
86					
87					
88					
89					
90					

Figure 2

Age	Premium	Interest	Cash Value	Income Distribution	Death Benefit
31	$10,000	6.6%	$5,845		$234,189
32	$10,000	6.6%	$15,723		$244,004
33	$10,000	6.6%	$26,281		$254,500
34	$10,000	6.6%	$37,573		$265,730
35	$10,000	6.6%	$49,654		$277,749
36	$10,000	6.6%	$62,580		$290,614
37	$10,000	6.6%	$76,580		$304,385
38	$10,000	6.6%	$91,648		$319,124
39	$10,000	6.6%	$107,915		$334,896
40	$10,000	6.6%	$125,719		$352,205
41	$10,000	6.6%	$144,739		$370,729
42	$10,000	6.6%	$165,055		$402,287
43	$10,000	6.6%	$186,744		$440,716
44	$10,000	6.6%	$209,405		$479,538
45	$10,000	6.6%	$233,647		$518,697
46	$10,000	6.6%	$259,966		$558,926
47	$10,000	6.6%	$288,105		$602,140
48	$10,000	6.6%	$318,179		$645,904
49	$10,000	6.6%	$350,323		$690,136
50	$10,000	6.6%	$384,675		$734,730
51	$10,000	6.6%	$421,385		$779,563
52	$10,000	6.6%	$460,648		$819,954
53	$10,000	6.6%	$502,652		$859,536
54	$10,000	6.6%	$547,606		$898,074
55	$10,000	6.6%	$595,724		$935,287
56	$10,000	6.6%	$647,206		$970,808
57	$10,000	6.6%	$702,253		$1,025,290
58	$10,000	6.6%	$761,123		$1,080,794
59	$10,000	6.6%	$824,090		$1,137,244
60	$10,000	6.6%	$891,455		$1,194,549
61	$10,000	6.6%	$963,540		$1,252,602
62	$10,000	6.6%	$1,040,600		$1,331,968
63	$10,000	6.6%	$1,122,991		$1,414,968
64	$10,000	6.6%	$1,211,097		$1,501,760
65	$10,000	6.6%	$1,305,319		$1,592,489
66		6.6%	$1,289,095	$100,000	$1,567,914
67		6.6%	$1,271,934	$100,000	$1,1554,499
68		6.6%	$1,253,773	$100,000	$1,539,034
69		6.6%	$1,234,543	$100,000	$1,521,351
70		6.6%	$1,214,185	$100,000	$1,501,285
71		6.6%	$1,192,633	$100,000	$1,478,659

Using Life Insurance for Retirement Income

72		6.6%	$1,170,127	$100,000	$1,433,381
73		6.6%	$1,146,724	$100,000	$1,383,156
74		6.6%	$1,122,535	$100,000	$1,327,764
75		6.6%	$1,097,710	$100,000	$1,266,997
76		6.6%	$1,072,445	$100,000	$1,200,653
77		6.6%	$1,045,799	$100,000	$1,181,654
78		6.6%	$1,017,607	$100,000	$1,161,480
79		6.6%	$987,703	$100,000	$1,139,981
80		6.6%	$955,917	$100,000	$1,117000
81		6.6%	$921,984	$100,000	$1,092,285
82		6.6%	$885,476	$100,000	$1,065,412
83		6.6%	$846,050	$100,000	$1,036,048
84		6.6%	$803,286	$100,000	$1,003,780
85		6.6%	$756,646	$100,000	$968,075
86		6.6%	$705,486	$100,000	$928,286
87		6.6%	$649,196	$100,000	$883,782
88		6.6%	$586,925	$100,000	$833,782
89		6.6%	$517,544	$100,000	$777,057
90		6.6%	$439,868	$100,000	$712,429

For more insight, you can also watch a short YouTube video explaining why the traditional retirement savings vehicles are not great for retirement savings.

https://youtu.be/kujLwfTTWIg

As you can see from figure 1, you would be out of money in the 13th year of retirement at age 78; and that is not considering any major losses due to market volatility. By the way, when I went to one of the major brokerage firm's website to do a retirement income calculation with these numbers, the final balance they estimated in savings at age 65 is $482,000, which conveniently falls in line with the 4% withdrawal rule for retirement income plans. This would pay out a pathetic $1,609 per month or $19,308 per year for 25 years. My calculation ends with $1,351,260. Let us take taxes in account at 33%. That would leave $905,344. That still leaves you with a difference of $422,644. My question is, where is that $422,644 going? Could it be accounting for the fees to manage the account or could it be accounting for the fees plus anticipated losses? For argument's sake, let us just use my calculation for this comparison.

At the end of 35 years of saving $10,000 per year at a rate of 6.6% per year you would end up with $1,351,260. This individual would need anywhere from 85% to 150% of his $100,000 income he was earning. For simplicity let us use 100% which is the $100,000. Pulling out $100,000 per year in retirement, he would end up running out of money in year 13. As you can see due to taxes, he is not getting that $100,000 He is left with $67,000 at a 33% tax rate. Who knows if this will be the tax rate or at that time. Many believe that it will be higher in the future. This is another negative aspect of using these traditional retirement savings vehicles. If taxes are higher in the future, then you would have to pay the tax rate at that time.

Now let us look at figure 2 in the life insurance policy at the same rate at the age of 65. He has $1,305,319 taking out that same $100,000 over the next 25 years. He gets the full $100,000 due to no taxes being paid, and he does not run out of money in this scenario. At the end of the 25 years at age 90, he has pulled out $2,500,000. Should he die at age 90, he would still have left $712,429 to transfer to his beneficiary. So, what is the difference between the two strategies? Why does one run out of money and the other takes more money out, does not run out of money, and have over $712,000 to pass on to his beneficiary? The two major differences are no taxes are being taken from the life insurance policy, and secondly, the policy continues to grow interest while he is taking money out for retirement income. The policy continues to grow interest because the money is not invested in the stock market. It continues to safely earn a good rate of return with the life insurance company.

So, here is my question to you. Which one would you rather have? Would you rather run out of money before you die? Or would you rather pull out $2,500,000 and still have over $712,000 to transfer to your beneficiary? I am sure you can see the answer is quite clear. You can do this comparison yourself by going to one of the major brokerage firm's website and do a retirement income calculation by filling in the numbers. Then ask a life insurance agent or broker to run an illustration with the same interest rate. You could also reach out to us for consultation and we could do that for you.

Chapter 12

Using Life Insurance for Wealth Transfer

When the average person talks about creating and building generation wealth they usually don't think life insurance. They do not know that they can buy it. I too was one of those people until I learned how wealthy individuals and wealthy families have been using life insurance to transfer and increase their wealth from generation to generation, for many, many years! What you must understand though, is even though the wealthy have been using this strategy for many, many years, it is not just reserved for them. Now that you understand the strategies, you too can use life insurance not only to create, but to build generational wealth. Many families in the past have passed on money whether through life insurance or other financial vehicles, yet it does not result in generational wealth; why is this? This is because they do not have a system as to how that money will be utilized and what to do to grow it continuously. Think about it, how many people have you heard about winning the lottery and got millions of dollars, and within five years they were broke again. This is the danger of passing on and just splitting up money amongst your heirs. If their relationship with money is to spend it, then that money will be gone in no time. It does not matter how much money one has. If it is not placed into a system to work, grow, and multiply, it will eventually run out! That is why when you talk about passing on generational wealth, it is important to understand that it is not only the money that you pass along. You need to pass along the mindset, the knowledge, the principles, habits, and strategies to your heirs so they know how to operate without you being here.

Take the Vanderbilt family, for example. In the late 1800s, they were the wealthiest family in the United States of America. However, after amassing significant wealth, by the third generation, it began to decimate. This was mainly due to philanthropy and lavish spending. They did not have a system in place to continue growing their wealth. As I mentioned earlier, if you do not have a system in place designed to continue to grow and multiply wealth, then it does not matter how much you have, at some point it will run out! Giving away the money and spending it lavishly without having a vehicle and a system to keep and build on the wealth you create, then the result is what happened; it runs out!

As of 2023, there is not much to show for the wealth that the Vanderbilt family had built. The Rockefeller family on the other hand, are still one of the wealthiest family in the world today. It is not publicly known just how wealthy they are because all their wealth is locked in into trusts, which gives them total privacy. They have a trust committee that manages and oversees the wealth to make sure that it is maintained and kept properly. They combined life insurance with trusts by putting life insurance on each generation and having the trusts as the beneficiaries so that all the death benefit from each generation continues to go back into the family trusts. Family members will have access to the trusts, but money is just not given out to the next generation; like is typically done when wealth is transferred. This has proven to be a great strategy because it gives family members access but does not give them entitlement. With the trust committee in place, anyone within the family who wants to access the money must get approval from the trust committee. They operate the funds in their trusts like a banking system. Therefore, family members have access to borrow from the trusts, but they would pay it back. So, with life insurance death benefit proceeds going back into the trusts and family members putting back money that they borrowed, the trusts never run out of money!

If there is one thing, we can all learn from the Rockefellers is their system of keeping and maintaining their wealth. It has proven over time, that it's a system that works; and it is a system designed to maintain and grow generational wealth. At this point, this cannot be disputed; it works! Not only did they know how to make their money; once they made it, they knew exactly what to do to keep it and grow it long term as well. In the bestselling book, What Would the Rockefellers Do, author Garrett B. Gunderson laid out the system that they used to maintain their wealth using life insurance and trusts, and showed you how you could follow the same concept, and create a system like the Rockefeller system for your family. I would recommend that if you want to set up a trust, you seek a trust attorney or someone that specializes in preparing trusts. For life insurance you should seek a broker or agent that is familiar with this type of structure and who has access to the right companies that will make your policy work efficiently. If you need help with the life insurance side, our team could also help you.

To fathom how your money could grow exponentially from generation to generation, it is important to understand the rule of 72. Italian mathematician, Luca Pacioli, is credited with discovering the rule of 72 and it was championed by Albert Einstein. It states that when you divide 72 by the interest rate, it will tell you the number of years it takes for your money to double. So, let us examine how that would look with a permanent life insurance policy. Let us say an individual, I will call John, has a policy that he started funding in his earlier years, and was able to fund his policy with $500,000 by age 40. The interest rate we will use here is 6%, which is normal. So, 72 divided by 6, and your answer is 12. Which means it will take 12 years for that half a million dollars to double. At age 52 John will have $1,000,000. At age 64 John's money will grow to $2,000,000. At age 76 it will grow to $4,000,000, and at age 88 it will grow to $8,000,000. This is the power of compounding interest. The money keeps doubling from the new principal. So, the more it doubles the bigger it gets, and the bigger it gets, the more it doubles! John will have over $8,000,000 to transfer to his heirs, assuming he dies at or before age 90. What do you suppose his heirs should do with that $8,000,000? You guessed it right, follow the same blueprint and do the same thing that John did to amass that amount. Now they have a significantly larger amount to start with. This is only going to continue to grow generation after generation. Now, if John uses his cash value for retirement income, then he will have less than $8,000,000 to transfer. Still, he would be funding the policy with $500,000, use a lot more than $500,000 for retirement income, and transfer a lot more than $500,000 to his heirs. Which other financial vehicle do you know of that you can safely execute what I just explained? I challenge you to come up with one.

I hope you are excited, and you see how a system like this could make a huge difference in your family legacy for generations to come! Now you may be saying, I do not have that much money to create such a plan. That is not the right mindset to have. It is not about the amount of money that you have. It is about the concept. The concept still works; whether you can fund a policy with $5,000 a year or $50,000 a year, it does not matter! What is important is that you start from where you are, while time is on your side. You can always add more policies, in the future, as you increase your capital throughout the process. Now that you have the information, I hope you take it upon yourself to be the one that will utilize it to change your family's legacy, and start the process of building long term generational wealth. I hope this project gave you some insight on the power of being a policy owner of a permanent life insurance contract, and I hope it will inspire you to take immediate action! Good luck with your journey of buying and building generational wealth.

For additional resources you can find me at the following social media platforms.

Facebook: https://www.facebook.com/courtney.beckles

Instagram: https://instagram.com/blackstallion_insurancebroker

LinkedIn: https://www.linkedin.com/in/courtney-beckles-235975200

YouTube Channel: https://youtube.com/channel/UCye6zHEIixLW0yaNoEazVcw

Join a community of individuals using life insurance to build generational wealth:
https://www.facebook.com/groups/1242802146617215/

Book a free life insurance consultation with myself of a member of my team:
https://www.calendbook.com/cbeckles27/lifeinsuranceconsultation

ABOUT THE AUTHOR

Courtney Beckles was born in Kingston Jamaica and attended the prestigious St. Georges College in Kingston, Jamaica. His family migrated to Paterson, New Jersey, USA in 1992 and he finished high school at John F. Kennedy H.S. in Paterson. It was challenging for Courtney to adapt to a new country, with a new climate, new environment, and no friends. Soon after he joined the track and field team and gained some new friends. He first exhibited his leadership qualities as the captain of the track and field team. He excelled in his role, but unfortunately his track and field aspirations were cut short by a very serious hamstring tear. He would then turn his attention to the workforce.

His career journey started as a retail manager where he worked for large retailers such as Footlocker, Bed Bath & Beyond, and Staples. It is during his time in this industry that he developed customer service, sales, and operational skills, and enhanced leadership skills; which he was able to transfer into the financial services industry. After experiencing burnout, it was time for a career change. He transitioned into the banking and insurance industry where he worked as a bank manager, as well as a life insurance producer. he later added credit repair, rebuilding, and restoration to his toolbox. His experience in this industry, as well as going through his own financial challenges; including going through a foreclosure, energized him into making financial literacy a priority in his life. This decision has made a tremendous impact in his life, and he is committed to making it a permanent lifestyle. He is very passionate about what he does because he knows what financial literacy did for him, and what it can do for others, especially the youths. Recently, he accomplished a goal of going back to his high school and speaking to the students about financial literacy. The students really appreciated it, and it gave him more fulfillment than any work he has ever done for pay.

Entrepreneurship is something that was always within him. He tried entrepreneurship twice before, but went back to the workforce after failing to figure it out. In January of 2021, he finally decided to go into business for himself; and June of 2023 make 7+ years that he has been in the Life Insurance business. The information he learned about the ins and outs of the life insurance industry has helped him develop a passion for helping people. According to Courtney, the way the information is delivered to consumers is usually for the professional's benefit, and not the client. This is why his focus is to educate his clients on how life insurance products can work for them.

His mission is to make sure his clients have a good understanding of life insurance in general, and specifically how the solutions they choose will help them achieve their financial goals. He believes there should be full transparency; no secret! He advocates that agents and brokers alike need to be fully transparent about the pros and cons of every solution they offer a client. He makes sure his clients fully understand what they are buying. He states "too often I come across people who buy life insurance policies and put them away and do not really understand what they bought." Courtney and his team is doing everything they can to combat these issues. He believes clients should understand what they buy, and clearly see how it will help them achieve their goals. His policies are written with the client's benefits in mind 100% of the time.

About the Author

He credits any success he has in the life insurance industry to having the mindset of helping clients win!

These days his goal is to help small businesses and individuals, and real estate investors create and build wealth through life insurance, as well as learning how to leverage credit. This will empower them with the knowledge and resources to get their finances in order early in the game, and avoid some of the mistakes he made earlier in his life. His work also gives him the opportunity to do his part in helping his community become financially literate; which is very important to him. He looks forward to the continued journey, and hopes you will join him! He can be found on the following social media platform: Facebook: Courtney Beckles

Instagram: blackstallion_insurancebroker

YouTube: blackstallion_insurancebroker

LinkedIn: Courtney Beckles

Made in the USA
Middletown, DE
29 August 2023